CAN YOU COPY CAT?

CAN YOU COPY CAT?

Dr. Brett Long, D.C.

pediatric chiropractor

gatekeeper press™
TAMPA, FLORIDA

The views and opinions expressed in this book are solely those of the author and do not reflect the views or opinions of Gatekeeper Press. Gatekeeper Press is not to be held responsible for and expressly disclaims responsibility of the content herein.

Can You Copy Cat?

Published by Gatekeeper Press

7853 Gunn Hwy., Suite 209
Tampa, FL 33626

www.GatekeeperPress.com

Copyright © 2023 by Dr. Brett Long, D.C.

All rights reserved. Neither this book, nor any parts within it may be sold or reproduced in any form or by any electronic or mechanical means, including information storage and retrieval systems, without permission in writing from the author. The only exception is by a reviewer, who may quote short excerpts in a review.

.

Library of Congress Control Number: 2022951964

ISBN (hardcover): 9781662935312

ISBN (paperback): 9781662935329

eISBN: 9781662935336

DEDICATION

To my wife Bailey for always motivating me to do my best, as well as my two sons Adler and Everett for inspiring me to write this book.

I hope that this book will help future generations avoid unnecessary lower back pain, which is the number one cause of disability worldwide.

DISCLAIMER PAGE

During each movement have the child move slowly and focus on form. At no point should they hold their breath or feel pain of any kind. If there is pain during the movement, you should consult with a pediatric chiropractor for a proper evaluation.

Chiropractic care using gentle pediatric adjusting techniques
has been shown to help infants with the following:

- Constipation
- Colic & fussiness
- Abnormal crawl/gait
- Behavioral issues
- Torticollis

- Latching issues
- Tongue-tie symptoms
- Improved immunity
- Ear infections
- Reflux

Cat woke up with a twist in his spine.

He perched and then stretched, but it hurt him this time.

"Arching my back up while looking down is my go-to move.

If I can't do that, what else can I do . . . ?"

Can you copy cat?

Cat: Starting on all fours, put your head down while arching your back up with hips and tailbone tucked in. Your body should look like an upside-down "U" shape.

The wise old cow chimed in, knowing just what to do.

"First, put your chest out and chin up, then let out your best MOO!

Push down into the ground, back flat as a table,

knees and toes pointed down, keeping you stable."

Can you copy cow?

Cow: Starting out on all fours lift your head up, stick your chest out, and keep your back flat with shoulders pulled back.

First thing in the morning, even dog knows to stretch.

Right after he makes his dog bed, but before he plays fetch . . .

"I lower my head down and lift my tail up to the sky.

Then I breathe in and then out, letting out a big doggy sigh!"

Can you copy dog?

Dog: Starting on all fours, curl your toes up and push them into the ground while you lift your bottom up to the sky as if someone is pulling your tail up. Next, push off the ground with your hands and make sure you feel the stretch along the back of your legs.

Cat paid a visit to the small bunny rabbit,

who said his routine starts with this one healthy habit.

"After I wiggle my tail and open my eyes,

I squat down to the ground and then jump really high!"

Can you copy rabbit?

Rabbit: Stand with feet shoulder-width apart, making sure that your weight is on the heels of your feet and not your toes. Next, stick your bottom out backwards as you bend your hips and knees, lowering yourself to the ground. Keep your eyes looking straight ahead when lowering yourself and try not to let your knees go in front of the toes.

The cat was happy that he no longer felt a twist in his back.

Doing all the different stretches together, made it feel like that.

Now cat knows that to keep having fun,

he needs to stretch like ALL the animals . . .

What's your favorite one?

Dr. Brett Long is a pediatric chiropractor and father of two boys under two years old. He knows from his private practice and personal experience, the importance of proper movement. On a daily basis, he sees the end result of improper movement patterns in his office.

Dr. Long was inspired to take a proactive approach. Rather than waiting for you or your children to end up in his office with back pain, he'd author a series of books to educate young readers and their parents on simple movements they can practice at home. When these fundamental motor skills are practiced and taught at an early age, the child possesses a strong foundation of skills they can continue to build on the rest of their life.